"Are we ready to go?" asked Flora.

"Nearly," said Mum.

Their sleeping bags, food and a tent were squashed into the car. Dad kissed Flora goodbye.

3

Mum and Flora noticed cows and sheep grazing in green fields. They saw the sea sparkling. Then they spotted the campsite sign!

Camping this way

The Jumpy Bumpy Feeling

Written by Jenny McLachlan

Illustrated by Anna-Lena Kühler

RISING ★ STARS

Have you ever been camping? Flora wanted to go camping more than anything in the world, and today, her mum was taking her!

Flora helped Mum put up the tent. It took a long time, and Mum got a bit grumpy.

Flora loved it inside the blue tent because she felt as if she was under the sea. The tent had lots of pockets instead of cupboards. Flora put her socks in one pocket and her very precious duck in another.

"Is it time to go to bed?" asked Flora.

"We haven't had dinner yet," laughed Mum.

Flora explored while Mum cooked dinner.
She watched some children flying a kite, and
discovered a big tyre swing hanging from a tree.

Flora and Mum ate their dinner sitting in canvas deckchairs.

"Is it time to go to bed?" asked Flora.

"Nearly!" said Mum.

Mum took Flora to the bathroom to brush her teeth.

The campsite bathroom was very different to the bathroom at home. Cobwebs dangled from the lights, and the floor was muddy. It made Flora feel funny inside.

When Flora was tucked up in her sleeping bag, Mum read her a story. But when she switched off the torch, everything went very dark.

"Oh!" said Flora.

"I'm still here," said Mum's shadow.

Flora wished she had her night-light with her.

Flora couldn't fall asleep. The tent was too dark. The sleeping bag was too slippery. The airbed was too bouncy.

Worst of all, Flora was wearing socks to keep her feet warm. Flora never wore socks in bed at home. The funny feeling inside got bigger.

Then, Flora heard a snuffle outside the tent.
Was it an escaped beast? The snuffle gave
Flora a horrible jumpy, bumpy feeling inside.

"Mum!" she cried. "Everything is different. I want to go home!"

Mum took Flora outside and wrapped her arms around her.

Together, they saw that the snuffling was a horse in the next field. They saw the sky was full of glittering stars. They saw bats flitting past.

"It's normal to miss home," whispered Mum.
"It can feel strange when things are different.
But it can feel exciting too."

Up in a tree, an owl hooted. Flora never heard
owls hooting at home. Excited shivers ran down
her back. Maybe she would be able to get to sleep
after all ...

The next morning, Mum made Flora a chocolate spread sandwich for breakfast. Flora never had chocolate spread sandwiches for breakfast at home.

Later, Flora played with the children, making kites swoop in the cloudless sky.

Then Mum pushed her on the tyre swing, sending her as high as the trees. Flora felt so jumpy and bumpy inside that she couldn't stop laughing.

"Do you still want to go home?" said Mum.

"No way!" said Flora. "But next time we go camping, let's bring Dad and Nell too, just to make it feel a bit more like home."

Talk about the story

Answer these questions:

1 Why did Flora love being inside the blue tent?

2 Why did Flora wish she had her night-light?

3 Why couldn't Flora fall asleep at bedtime?

4 Why do you think Mum whispered on page 15?

5 Is 'The Jumpy Bumpy Feeling' a good title for this story? Why or why not?

6 What gives you a jumpy bumpy feeling? Who makes you feel better?

Can you retell the story in your own words?